Anything on Earth

Anything on Earth

poems by
Ken Weisner

Hummingbird Press
Santa Cruz, California

Acknowledgment is gratefully made to the following periodicals, in the pages of which many of these poems first appeared: *Bathyspheric Review*, "The Ocean as a Symbol of Compassion"; *Black Zinnias*, "Reply to Rimbaud," "Lyric"; *The Clarinet*, "Anything on Earth"; *Good Times*, "Creation," "Ghazal," "Flesh Music," "Spring Retreat"; *Poets Against the War Website*, (http://www.poetsagainstthewar.org/displaypoem.asp?AuthorID=17120), "After Gertrude Stein," "You Rise in Us, Donald Rumsfeld"; *Porter Gulch Review*, "The Beauty of Work as a Boy," "Bee Tree," "Echo Space," "The Empire of His Will," "The Gardener," "Dear Maude," "Youngest," "Your California"; and *Santa Cruz Weekly*, "Indian Summer."

Library of Congress Control Number: 2010922761

ISBN: 9780-9792567-5-2

Cover photos by Ken Weisner
Cover design by Kathleen Roberts

HUMMINGBIRD PRESS
2299 Mattison Lane
Santa Cruz, CA
95062-1821

Printed in USA

This collection would not exist without the love, music, green thumb, and culinary art of Kit Birskovich; the energy and wisdom of James and Matthew, our sons; and the nurturance of the poetry comrades, especially those among my friends, colleagues, poetry group, and Hummingbird Press who read and commented on this manuscript during one or more of its phases: Shirley Ancheta, Len Anderson, Charles Atkinson, Marilyn Chin, Dave Denny, Bob Dickerson, Suzanne Helfman, Rosie King, Paul Kolhoff, Stephen Kuusisto, George Lober, Tilly Shaw, Roz Spafford, Debra Spencer, David Sullivan, Jeff Tagami and Amber Coverdale Sumrall. Amber's writing retreats at the New Camaldoli Hermitage in Lucia, Big Sur, inspired first drafts of many of these poems. Thanks to other dear friends/readers, including Julia Alter, Barbara Bloom, Lorraine Birskovich, Joanna Martin, Lara Owen, Marilyn Patton, Maggie Paul, Sarah Rabkin, Dana Wendt, and Gary Whittington. Appreciation to Ellen Bass, Dorianne Laux, Joe Millar and Robert Bly for inspiration at Esalen and Asilomar; to Poetry Santa Cruz; also to Nils Peterson for multifaceted poetic leadership and energy—and Maureen Draper for including "Under the Piano" in her 2007 *Music Lovers' Poetry Anthology*, making possible many wonderful readings. Thanks to choreographer Robert Battle and those others who performed "After Gertrude Stein" at Uppity Theater in Saint Louis in 2004, and to John Chandler and Wilma Marcus Chandler who included "I Am No Sufi" and "The Builder" in Willing Suspension Armchair Theater's 2009 presentation of *Lost and Found: The Literature of Fathers and Sons* at the Actors' Theatre in Santa Cruz. Appreciation to Al Young who posted "For John Lovas, Final Boarding" at alyoung.org in 2008. Thanks to the devoted interest and support of my brothers Tom and Stan and their families; Stan & Connie also accommodated an indispensable annual writing week at Truckee. This volume remembers Frank Birskovich, Susan and Al Crawford, Lucille Clifton, Kathleen Flowers, Donald Justice, John Lovas, Morton Marcus, Maude Meehan, Christine Mergozzi, Jean Miller, James O'Keefe, Doug Virostko, Irv Weisberg, Ruth Weisner, Gilbert Weisner, and the others who came before.

CONTENTS

I

The Empire of His Will

Six Meditations for George W. Bush

I
Consider: he was once an innocent boy—
so sleepy in his cowboy suit!
Then, too suddenly,
tangled by that cruelest master, history:
its brutal par fives—its smoky limos
and scary private schools.

II
Be humane. Seek to heal his addiction:
the alcoholism. Ask:
what will bring him closer to God and to himself?
The hairshirt of unemployment?
The cleansing purity
of life on the ranch? Visualize this.

III
Or ponder his dyslexia
so long denied! Be honest with yourself:
he needs more time
for Laura to read to him!

IV
Now reflect upon his shame—
and forgive him for repressing it.
After all, you're glad it wasn't you—
graduating from everywhere, including Yale,
without deserving it—and everybody knew.

V
If you feel anger, this is normal.
Take a cleansing breath.
And, as Shakespeare would, be compassionate
to a boy thrust outside himself,
like a puppet on a throne.

VI

So wish him well—wish him revelation.
Meanwhile, in November, lift his hand with God's hand
from the trigger.
Back in Texas, in your mind,
tuck the sweet boy in.

6/04

Rage

I've seen rage—
seen it catch a house afire
just like that—the walls ablaze.
Seen children woken from their sleep
or frozen to their beds—
bottles fly, glasses break—
and the ghost of some ancient wounded father
pulse in the home fire coals,
limbic alarm that sweeps like a hand
across a table, a face,
before the hand can think:
explosive—not an avalanche,
but flame with accelerant,
head like a mop-soaked wick
down the throat of a cocktail
bomb.... You can't put it out
with water, with words; can't tell
the anger from the shame, fire
from fuel.
The new day
will chill to a tousled, sleepy
head—could be anybody's home,
anybody's room—almost all the ash,
the ruin, kept within.
There's a haunted, burnt-out
house upon the flood.
And that's not the worst of it—
the worst of it's the fear,
how everyone agrees,
relieved by silence:
nothing happened here.

You Rise in Us, Donald Rumsfeld

Who feels road rage,
perhaps, on a sunny day in spring—

fantasizes what he'd do to the rapist
if he caught him—

who feels these things
was surely a child once.

And so we know Donald well
and stroke his forehead like a boy,

and say *yes, yes; of course, Donald.*
You're fine. You're really doing fine.

And there is no shame
in the wish to invade,

but equally, one would suppose,
nothing wrong with knowing

that we must not—
because, *Donald, there is*

higher authority: our statesmen, our legislators,
our ambassadors, our best minds,

all of whom can protect us, Donald,
from what he is—and what you are,

and from how you rise in us predictably,
with your Mephisophelean charm:

witty, making promises, smirking
with a little righteousness,

practicing all the clarity and diction
you picked up along the way; at last you are righting

all the wretched wrongs
of the schoolyard. *Ah, what was done to you!*

We understand, for you rise in us, too, Donald,
like a fantasy of revenge, and are part of us,

and are only kept in check
and balance by our knowing what you are

and how you must be kept down
in good times and in bad.

For you are already
seething in each of us,

the face like a skull,
the grin barely withheld, the shiver of pleasure

at each dark pronouncement.

The Empire of His Will

I
I could stand all morning at the sink
with the red haired boy
who couldn't stop brushing his teeth or
combing his hair or washing his hands and face

and what could scare a person most
besides the lobster hands—
to watch him lather, shave... lather, shave—
was the brightness in his eyes;

where was impatience, rage?
He couldn't stop or leave,
or touch the handle "just right enough"
to walk through the door.

I waited for emotions,
but somehow, as the hours passed,
earnest, dutiful, business-like,
he'd let me gently push him through each task.

II
Today I'd like to see him once more,
his obscene patience and humility,
and tell him how I am caught sometimes—
staring at the clock mornings,

waiting for 7:02 or 7:05, far luckier than 7:01 or 7:06—
it's a trick I know—no matter how bleak,
who's dying... you need me to explain?
I can climb up into the world

from the ladders numbers provide.
Or the boxes of stuff, the clippings I can't discard—
who am I without these? I keep
moving to throw them away,

but my hand pulls back. I get through
by holding on—things, habits… lies….
Or it gets out of hand, the gene.
And one day the halls are lined with old newspapers.

The streets are lined with soldiers…
I need a drink… and it's no longer grace,
this need for order, controlled
by our own desire to control.

III
No matter what the boy did,
he couldn't enter the next room…
in his inner-theater of pleasure gone awry,
stuck in bathrooms,

standing at the doors of the world,
always preparing,
never prepared enough.
I remember his courage; he trusted others,

took their advice, never hurt anyone,
even strapped to electroshock gurneys
or toxic regimens, so good…
he just took the whole crazy thing in.

IV
Why leave this bed, this room?
I think of a boy who couldn't leave at all—swallowed by
the empire of his will.

I wait for the next auspicious
numeral to appear
on the alarm's digital face.

Any numeral will do.

Contemplation

New Camaldoli Hermitage, Lucia, 2004

Walk through
night,
stare down fears,
protected

by a language that has
but one letter in its alphabet,
a letter that defines
space and everything else,

sharpened like
a good shovel—
skeleton key
on the nape of sunset,

consonant
that seeds the fruit of OM.

What happens
to the unafraid?
Do they forget
their fear,

grief,
blindness—
forget
the only thing they know?

Take their own eyes out
in favor of their hands?
Meaning
has its own dark language.

Over and over, the journey
begins.

Melisma

for Sam Cooke

I

I heard The Soul Stirrers in my car today
asking someone to wash away their burdens:
"Kno-o-o-o-o-ow there's consolation,

as long as I know you're there,"
and later, "while I'm traveling he-e-e-e-re alone"—
Five syllables as in: *a lonely place*

that may require a seemingly infinite
patience and resolve. We pluck words from history
but incarnate them with our music,

float them out like birds or dolphins
into the blood of the ear.
No point in singing otherwise.

Meaning is a *gospel* thing.
The ghost of intention
across the cool sleeve of the voice....

If you want me to see, to feel,
then let me hear your voice trying
to understand what a single word means.

II

So around 1949 he's in Memphis
in a park with some girls. A white park.
And he gets beaten

badly. A white park was a white park
in the book of Memphis.
And not much had changed

in 1963, when arrested for disturbing the peace
for trying to *check into a hotel*
in Shreveport, he writes:

"It's been a lo-o-o-ong time coming,
but I know a change is gonna come."
And you know what he means:

"'Wait' has almost always meant 'Never.'"

III
"It's been too hard living, but I'm afraid to di-i-i-i-ie."
Maybe the puritanicals, the dualists,
the racists, are too tone deaf to cross over,

to slide over, to think over anything—
they may prefer the written-out syllables
of Glo-o-o-o-o-oh—o-o-o-o-oh—o-o-o-o-oh-ria,

ecstatic birth, an elevator nativity tune.
But I'm sticking with Sam, who kept on living
after his country, after his baby drowned,

until he was shot in early '65—
before enough change had "co-o-ome."
That's three syllables: *arrival, living or dead, despite despair.*

Youngest

I'm the youngest;
my brothers are away.
It's 1964; my father is doing
business in Japan.

The concrete floor
of our house in the hills
is warm where the pipes come
close to the surface.

And sometimes ants pour through
a fissure in the floor
where the earth has settled,
and I follow their trails

forward to their worship idols:
a crumb, or a cat bowl filled
with liver flavored goo,
nearly limitless resource,

and lie on my side like Gulliver
and watch for a long time,
their individual glory, their
efficiency, their bursts of panic

when I intercede with the slightest breath
or shadow of a hand closing in.
Otherwise, they continue to stay in line
and mine with intricate single-mindedness.

Such opportunists! Do they ever sleep?
It's mid-winter, but the floor is warm
and my mother will not be awake
for a while yet, with a chore for me:

Antrol, Raid, paper towels—and a broom.
Oh, the tens of thousands of corpses!
The chaos that sets in
when I spray,

wipe them up like mud,
flush them away.
So in these early hours
I give them a little reprieve

and follow them through the house
a while and wonder at the idea
of a hundred thousand anything
just inches away each night

from our sleeping mouths,
doing their work,
so easily destroyed—
because small enough to massacre—

but ready to come again forever,
uninvited, and to win,
no less, to win the whole
thing—game, set, match—

in their own sweet time.

Ghazal

I am told it's good to forgive.
So I will do myself later and start with Dick Cheney.

After all, I honestly wept for Frankenstein.
Perhaps I can love Dick Cheney.

Doris Lessing says forgive what you cannot understand.
I will try not to understand Dick Cheney.

The lamby-soul of a child is sweet, androgynous.
So must be the soul of Dick Cheney.

Sometimes I am overcome that he is cynical.
I must not project my shadow onto you, Dick Cheney.

Did you ever truly clear a decent shelter for sorrow?
Me neither, Dick Cheney.

But I try. And in trying now, my hate
is turned to this flower, Dick Cheney.

If I knew you better—if you were a friend,
how much harder it would be, Dick Cheney,

to be tender and awake in the face of you.
It's easier to forgive people like Judas, Pharaoh, Dick Cheney,

than the people I know who voted for you,
some twice; some even with yard signs, Dick Cheney.

Why should it be your fault that you are so beloved?
We lifted the sedan chair, crowned you twice, Dick Cheney.

Then why does my body convulse
every time I think of your smile, Dick Cheney?

That would be judgment, I know.
I'm trying to forgive you, Dick Cheney,

to take you back to the many-armed sea of mothers
where you are unborn once more, Dick Cheney,

no pacemaker, no surgeons starting your heart
over and over, Dick Cheney;

no pesky Congress, no courts or lesbian daughter to ponder.
Just that bliss of androgynous innocence we all lost once, Dick Cheney.

Ken says *ah*, source of all beauty, still unborn sleep that lasts forever—
thing all music longs for, even yours, even mine, Dick Cheney.

After Gertrude Stein

I

Therefore is so certain, therefore
we invade them, therefore knowing
what we do, invade them, knowing
certain we are knowing,
knowing and invading, certain
knowing, certain, and certain, therefore—

so we knew therefore, and
in knowing, certain,
we invaded in our knowing,
we invaded in our therefore,
so, in springtime, so, in springtime
so, in therefore, therefore, springtime—

we invaded in our knowing
in our knowing we invaded,
certain were we, and it started
in our knowing, in our therefore
and it started in our knowing, then.
How frightened and alone in therefore

were we when we knew in springtime.
How frightened and alone and young,
in our therefore; in our knowing,
we were certain, oh, we were brave,
in our knowing, in our springtime—
who could tell us we weren't knowing?

We were certain, we were brave,
brave in springtime, brave in therefore,
we were frightened, we were brave,
invaded therefore, certain, knowing,
invaded young, invaded knowing,
invaded therefore, invaded springtime.

II
And it was goodness,
        it was language
told us goodness
        told us fight it
told us it was good to fight it,
        and it was language
told us fight it
        told us twice, fight it
fight it
        and it, was them
the language told us,
fight them, it told us.
        It was them, it told us.
It was a word,
        the word was it
and it was it, and it was them.
And it was them
        that fought it,
it was them alone that fought it,
        it alone,
but also them;
        he was good
we heard his language.
        It was evil, it was them...
and it was goodness
        it was language
told us goodness
        told us fight it,
told us it was good to fight it,
        and it was language
told us fight it
        told us twice, fight it
fight it, told us it was good
        to fight it.

3/4/03

II

Your California

Wrong Country

Sometimes you're the life, sometimes the sacrifice.
Marilyn Chin, "Turtle Soup"

It started out with
neighbors, regular folks, giving in
to thugs. Then Great Grandmother
a dour ghost in black lambswool,
her heavy black oak
furniture shipped over the Atlantic,
and my tiny grandfather
in suspenders and oversized trousers
in an overstuffed arm chair.
Out of fear, he never drove
in America, dreaming in German
for the rest of his life. I came of age
when his stomach cancer had already won
and my own father was also dying—
he who needed something other than war,
but got mostly war followed by
deal-makers and get-ahead racists
who kicked and buoyed him
even as he went into insulin shock
pushing the NURSE light
until his heart cramped.
In sum, the legacy was: scared
before, scared after.

A whole middle act
involves upwardly mobile parents,
a better neighborhood,
a whiter school—
but deep down, who really wants
a whiter school?

I am born to exiles who insist
on an English-speaking home.

I don't even realize my parents have accents
until my friends tell me, or that we're Jews
until we argue about it
when I'm eleven.

*

Today, although he died
when I was fourteen,
I still walk with my father
on 77th Avenue in East Oakland,
who turned shackles and turnbuckles
& giant spools of cable as tall as three men
—the kind of cable that sings, holds you aloft
when you drive out over the water—
who never graduated high school
but gradually turned it all into
white shirts, import/export, Japan—
United Airlines, 100,000-mile club...
higher educations for his sons.
My Viennese mother
went back to school.
But Dad could never afford it.

And although Lionel at the warehouse
always smelled like sweet liquor,
and sometimes Lou just didn't show,
mornings, back in the Tri-Metals Days,
my dad just bit his lower lip,
gave them their pay.
The furniture sorrowful and torn
like a tire shop, family run...

and although his hands were bitten
testaments of who-knows-what longing

endlessly deferred,
we were now washed clean with names
like "Tommy" and "Kenny"—
lifted into the conifered East Bay hills
where Joaquin Miller's hand-masoned towers
peer out over San Francisco Bay,

the great romantic West, the clear air—
not so much of lies, as erasures...
forgotten things—all that money,
white skin, and impeccable weather
make go away—and in his forties,
he's made it to his dream
home, though in his arthritic,
diabetic body, it's

still the wrong country—
a country we trade ourselves in for.

They gave us eyes
for injustice, our parents: how lies
become truths,
dividing city, nation, world, self;
how it could happen here—
and to fight it with every breath.

*

Still, today, I'd have a double bourbon with my father,
and after the rounds of hugs and smiles,
I'd let it be grim again.
Not because he's really gone—
but because of what most people
are willing to settle for—
what they're willing to do,

whom they're willing to kill,
and what they're willing to forget.

*

I saw my father pause and pace
at the synagogue door...
where my mother wouldn't have him go.
He wanted me to see this.
Neither had an answer. Either choice
was the wrong country.

Indian Summer

Santa Cruz, California

Everything is dying in the garden... only gourds still ripening,
and late tomatoes that keep filling with blood.
In the valley it's 105—a Salinan mirage—

a last stand slamming across the tile roofs of each mission.
So we pull off our shirts, sit on the patio
among the pumpkins and un-raked leaves—face the blazing lion.

"Western civilization is a temporary blip in the historical record..."
you say as you lay down your book, turn over to roast
a different continent of flesh. Eyes closed, you start to sweat.

"They say it's snowing in Boston." You turn again.
How utterly immoral... yet we always feign surprise.
And how we treasure it.

Salinan: Native Americans who lived in the Salinas Valley

Ranch Work

I was asked to dispatch them
as I saw fit—drowning worked well, I was told.
In free-love, anti-war northern California,
no one would have produced anything so connotatively disturbing
as a shotgun. And a humane injection, ether, chloroform?
A long and expensive drive to the vet? Not a chance.

So I collected three... unnamed, starving for love, grey and white,
crawling with fleas, matted hair where the scalp was oozing,
diseased, motherless... infected weepy eyes—a scourge
insinuating into campsite, sleeping bag,
summer kitchen. The health inspector

would arrive at any moment, and the children
tomorrow. One quick blow to the head
or twist of the neck?
I hadn't the nerve. Put all three in a bucket,
started filling with the hose.
Then a board over the top to hold them down.

But they pushed back, their bodies rigid, thrashing—
somehow finding air-pockets—
their jerky thumps and sloshing, electric.
They pressed and breathed against the board
or slipped around the shovel blade I tried next
to hold them under. Finally another bucket
to fit inside and seal the first.

Did it occur to me that water was already torture
to cats? I was doing as I was told.
Testosterone drenched—a mother's boy, almost fourteen.
Dave Conn, my brothers' friend—he never came home
from Vietnam. Each unwitting as a fetus
until I looked and saw the underwater scream.

Clear now as ever—a pair of eyes,
then a look that is weaker, the flame gone out.
Buried them like rats—with regret—but also pride
at having done a man's job.
Feral—untenable—everyone agreed
at this bonafide paradise: they had to go.

Your California

For Steven, 1957-2001

Twinge of bay laurel, savor of madrone, manzanita pasture,
horses still as stumps across the dry hills....
Once you were the glitter-eyed stranger
who stopped here just to point out to hikers
where the red-tails were nesting, the robin eggs were hidden,
or to make sure they'd see the King snake skin around the bend.
At sixteen years, with the squint of an old-timer,
you'd confess where the ripest blackberries were,
or warn of nettles, poison oak, a rocky slope—easy to fall a long way there.
I can never quite remember how to get to those places
where at night the stars are wild as the blackberries,
and you are naming them.
                    You were a connoisseur
of knowledge and esoteric talk. The storage locker
you left behind was one huge library—two thousand books.
Nevertheless, homeless, destitute, one winter night
in the groomed shrubbery behind a Las Vegas strip hotel...
two years since you pulled the trigger—
love gone awry, your past a choke-leash on your living
even though you had healed and served your time.

                    You'd stayed abandoned
in a labyrinth almost as horrible as your crime—
what fear and loneliness had spawned. Registered
as an offender. It was impossible
to find or keep the jobs you wanted, the friends:
to break through to a stable life.

And how to think of you now?
A bench, a plaque, another enclosure on your life?
like taking the pulsing flash, ever-shifting
fingerprint of a waterfall, and framing it behind ropes.
You had your share of that.
Steven, how do we hold these worlds together?

Now, on the roadside of any journey:
anonymous wild raspberries, purple blossomed thistle,
honeysuckle, fragrant mugwort, or against the dank path:
Solomon seal, licorice fern, medicinal oak. Anywhere I'm most
struck by nature's unfolding breeze or alphabet:
its runic stillness—each animal, each place.

All-Day Bus Trip to the Ashland Shakespeare Festival

Angel, our driver, is fabulous;
Dave, our trip leader, is an honorable man.
He had us vote on paper ballots
to choose a video for some on-board entertainment.
Macbeth won out over *Hamlet* and several comedies.
Who are these people who voted for *Macbeth*?
Ah, the tyranny of the majority! It's a beautiful sun-drenched day;
the bus filled with laughter and old friends...
and now for hour upon daylight hour,
wretched evil hatched out of lust, ambition, madness,
a thousand bloody daggers. Oh happy, happy vacation!

And from my seat in the back row left,
where I sat to a large degree out of chivalric politeness—
what reward but a grinding transmission and a chemical toilet?
Toil, trouble, and cauldron bubble...

Not that I nor sunny California deserves better, it occurs to me,
as I slump, give in, and gaze disgruntled out the filmy glass.
Each scorching degree of our fuel-drenched journey
pulls us through a curtained backdrop as of a rustic diorama,
yet a landscape of no small horror...
disturbing as any Shakespeare could imagine—
dragged now half-slumbering over wheel ruts of older roads:
colonial enslavers, arrogant landowners, rapacious loggers,
miners, and missionaries, or the vivid slit
throats (Miwok, Pomo, Wintu, Modoc),
ghosts: Chinese railroad workers, itinerant Filipinos,
and Japanese hauled off and robbed by the lawless state.

I think Macbeth is going mad now, Malcolm has withdrawn;
Dave and Angel announce we will stop soon for a little picnic
north of Sacramento—strip-malls, freeway, agribusiness to the horizon.

So just around the time Lady Macbeth starts to see things—
is it 100 degrees? we are offered rich food at table;
but I no longer see benign lunch meats laid before me,
and am reminded of many disturbing human truths and deadly hungers
right as we snap the group picture.

Why do I love the theater? Why have I come?
Oh, this is no Disneyland: no head-phoned, air-conditioned cocoon
can drown out what we've become. The sun is low;
Angel climbs the Siskiyou. The final dagger's in.

"Will these hands ne'er be clean," they say *(I'm sure of it now)*
as they leave the lavatory. They mumble to themselves,
but I can hear under their breath. *"What's done cannot be undone,"* I say
as they go by—and: "hold, enough" as they float by a second time.
They cannot close the door *fast* enough, it seems—
none of them, not one, not all my pretty ones.

All-You-Can-Eat

Scraping food off the smorgasbord rug
at Perry Boys, the all-you-can-eat joint,
the morning shift. I'd get down on my knees
with a knife where the patrons,
with massive, plodding feet,
had ground yesterday's meats, soups
and gravies into the carpet
—then my no-nonsense boss would have me
vacuum, clean windows,
even scrub baseboards
to honor the devoted
who would gather early
for our 10:00 AM opening,
looming clientele
lined up at the door for value—
their limited eye contact and
barely concealed sadness. All they could
forget. I kept the buffet cold
and wiped down spills,
the dressings and sauces—
refilled the tapiocas and jellos,
soda syrups and chocolate cakes,
but mostly back and forth between steam table,
scalding dish machine, and the sour dumpsters.
And it was hard to get far enough away
from those dumpsters. So afternoons,
I'd head straight to the ocean
at the foot of Woodrow,
to lie and read
in blistering sand, then baked
to a fine discomfort,
right at the point of agony,
dive into the rough break
and ask the sea to swallow me.

The Feet Are Giant-Hearted

I love the feel of duff, a forest floor
under my feet. Even at my urban workplace,
maybe walking with the administrative vice president
for budget and finance, I seek out the soft
shortcuts between asphalt paths, under redwoods,
along spongy berms, over wood chips, leaves, storm-tossed branches.
Some may look askance at this—a few feet of meadow?
four seconds of forest, a leafy patch of lawn....
Seed-pods catch—the trouser cuffs are wet;

it's a kind of memory. I provide the feet signals
like Anne Sullivan to Helen Keller—ecstatic indication
of dewy earth or moist dark leaves to awaken them
from what Thomas Merton called "the coma of the living"
—like letting the dog sniff around after all day cooped up in the house.

As from a screen porch into a spring rain—
it gives them hope that rises up from their pallid shoulders through
the whole nexus of interlocking joints and leg bones,
like fish thrown back into pond water.
The fact is, like Methuselah, the feet are giant-hearted
and have slept bravely for a long time;
they've been many things—emperors as well as slaves—
and have never forgotten hope, their fierce
passion, or the power and humility of their daily charge.

We are friends then. I only want to give them more
of what they deserve—each step, like each breath,
smuggled back from the paved world.
Or take the shoes off altogether,
ignore the head of marketing and the dean of institutional research
scowling a little from their office windows, heads tilted into the phone...
dressed impeccably behind steel and glass.
Ask your feet who you are—maybe they will tell you.

It Shouldn't Comfort You

We lay the tarp and wrestle in the Noble Fir;
straighten, position, water her body
wedged at its fresh cut ankle in a plastic anchor
that holds her upright with eight interior toggle screws;

there's not much bleeding due to the plastic caps—
they press hard, those steel fingers and thumbs
that lift and steady her trunk and graceful branches
in an upward flame, sconce for the torch of winter's darkest days.

We hold her here as an honored invocation.
If there is beauty it is of contrast:
we have destroyed her, and she is green;
we are warmed by her and we have destroyed her.

And so she floats there between life and death,
between our goodness and our ignorance, as we do,
shooting off light in all directions, bridging the dark
with light, the warmth of the body in space;

think of those moments when you know
who you are—a seed unfurls its truth:
it shouldn't comfort you, and yet it does; it is not comforting…
and yet, of an evening, it is—as true things sometimes are.

Scenes From a Marriage

She doesn't know how just to fall down the stairs.
She doesn't know how just to fall
without someone else having been negligent,
"I've been telling you for years
how slippery those stairs are..."

and although you care right away
about the bruises, the miracle
that she's otherwise OK, you fall short; you say,
"No you haven't; I never knew those stairs were..."
and lo, behold, tumbling...

"Five times" she has told you
"and how many more times
did I tell you we needed a banister there..."
"Or about that serpent in the orchard,
if I told you once, it was a hundred times..."

referring to her earlier fall into primal shame.
We don't know if she said
"Can you believe, Adam, I did that to myself?
—that I caused my own injury?
I am *such* a fool."

The problem is, if she did,
he probably said something mean like the cruel bastard
he had already become,
bang bang bang bang,
all the way down to the landing.

Playing the Mouthpiece

Beginner,/Perpetual beginner...

Theodore Roethke, "What Can I Tell My Bones"

After months of no time, I buzz my lips
and play arpeggios on the French horn mouthpiece;
to you it sounds as usual,
like a very old lady warming up her wavering, reedy voice
from a few rooms down the hall...
which has some hilarious truth to it—
as if instead of Prozac they gave out kazoos to cheer us.

It's a small sound, a bleating morning bird,
music *déshabillé,* primitive as grass,
anaphora in boxers and old undershirt,
unshaven pop, grandpa's suspenders.
Something as predictable as this!
The thing is, you've been suffering so long, the absurd
familiar song surprises you—what can you say?
makes everything that's wrong
suddenly ridiculous again, therefore loveable.

And any darkness closing in
collapses here in the face of this little transmutation,
dutifully modulating, inhabiting wheezy pipes,
working out the muscles of the face.
It tickles you—a form of revelation.
What is revealed—innocence, the gentleness
of the arch-enemy you can't live without—
the body, the world of others. How funny
all the hubris, art, and pretense of the world.
And as sometimes happens, you can't stop laughing—
it's the great tide of Boffo, carrying you away—
it's Dogberry, Bottom, Malvolio, Wall...

You can't hold back—the stomach muscles ache,
saying *stop, stop, please*—but all I have to do it seems,

is play the next arpeggios on the royal mouthpiece
hung with banners now in my imagination—
the normal warm-up fanfares—
and you're reduced to howls, breathless, primitive, kneeling,
asphyxiating as spasms can sometimes be.

And then I too am kidnapped by laughter,
by the power of this instrument—
just barely able to stop long enough to keep
entertaining you with more miniature fanfares,
and even though it hurts the stomach when you cannot stop—
mine too—and you need to throw up, and you carry
the wastebasket into the bathroom... but what could be funnier
than the sound of the beloved laughing
and throwing up and laughing some more,
and throwing up some more... and I become
stricken, doubled over in a paralysis
of spasm, struggling for breath now, on my knees—
because nothing could be funnier than this.

The Ocean as a Symbol of Compassion

The lantern fish of your desire, the prowling sharks,
the blood urchins, devil rays, perfect storms,
the inhuman, forbidding floor, its tangled wrecks and corpses,
infinite salt like so much cold steel,
and you, a bobbing cipher
in a Himalaya of waves,
in a Brobdingnagian vertigo so precipitous
you might as well be lost in space *and* time.
And then, to make matters worse,
the tender moorings, the shores
where love is made! Where life began!
The schoolchildren! The innocent at play!
Holy mother of obscene distances—mother of cold,
mother of dark, mother of death—perfect, compassionate one!

At the Potter's Wheel

Smudges, lids that squirrel, spouts
that don't cleanly pour, bowls that warp
no matter how she tries, always some
fleck of ash, faulty brew of glaze,
sticky, dangerous
placement in the kiln; each broken
piece, each loss troubling, the oven
not her own. Children in a chaotic world...
                                            yet always,
hunger for more. Sky carves its capillaries, trees
reach into stone, rain brings grief; hands
harvest river bottoms, spin and pull night-sky,
trace into being the spinning muck—
a lip, a mouth, a vase as high as her hips,
sun-scorched, beneficent, among siren veils of silt.

Lyric

Can I receive such a telegram? Compelled to utter
"Laila Heinonen," which leads to "Kirsi Taaminen"—
the first, a penpal with impeccable handwriting
(the photo she sent, sumptuous red haired Finn
in a short red dress: the knees of Laila Heinonen!
Her schoolgirl English! I was utterly dispatched
to bliss, a drowsy snow of half sleep,
as inside a glass globe, descending, to her)
or Taaminen—Kirsi—young cherry oak!
from the *Silja* line—its tabernacles of moonlight!
Early Baltic crossings, reindeer herds, harmonicas—
Wild bearded spruce! aphrodisiac guitars!
Decadent hives of neural firing—sex flowers—
gorgeous suspensions of dust in some feeding-frenzy of isolation!

Reply to Rimbaud

> *But the soul must be made monstrous.... The Poet makes himself a seer*
> *by a long, gigantic and rational derangement of all the senses.*
> Letter to Paul Demeny, 1871

No wonder you end up running guns.
Try working at one job, staying married,
staying put, being loyal to your immediate family,
not to mention in-laws. Not that I blame you
for a thing you did. Just don't tell me what a poet is.
Unspeakable torment... absolute faith... superhuman strength?
Well, OK, agreed. *Soaring among... ineffable and unnamable things?*
Fine, I'll go with that. *Visions?*—true enough.
But *madness?* Come on. And as for *unholiest damned,*
great criminal—swallowing every poison—
every form of love—Oh, please, Arthur! Maybe—maybe not.

Bee Tree

Let's compare them to ants. Or flies.
Love is the "birds and the bees," so where's the sing-song
for death—"The ants and the flies"? "The mold and the parasites"?
"The bacteria and the corpse-worms"?

The true test would be in the stench.
Tell me something beautiful about the smell of death,
especially those two or three weeks in summer
when you can't find the rodent rotting in the wall.

Consider it a rite of passage. You sit
in the smell of dead flesh. Meanwhile, these bees
are what got me started. They are visiting two trees:
a Chinese Scholar and a Chinese Tallow.

In the Scholar's case, this year the blossoms
have prolifically exuded and fallen in a puff of yellow sex.
So the bees are carpeting the fallen petals,
and the bees are winging through the dense, low crown.

You can step carefully and walk into the middle of this,
and they will leave you alone. Just watch so
none accidentally fly up your pants, and be advised
to wear shoes. True, I will have brought you here

in order for you to close your eyes and listen, but also to keep
them open and look around: you are ignored;
your smell is not interesting, not dead yet either.
Many would have you disappear now,

in favor of the bees who represent some force larger than
ourselves (I was going to say the universe!),
earnest, industrious—self-sacrificing—benign...
but then I would be leaving out

the whole controversy surrounding "Africanized"
aggressive behaviors reifying
racial stereotypes, creating fear—
and you were hoping

for lyric closure, and me too! So why am I the guy
who's still grim, even here in heaven?
Oh, fragrant Scholar! Something earned:
the sound, the vibration of summer.

The High Passes

You wonder if you'll ever make the lake.
You throw one foot out in front of the next.
It began at the trailhead, raucous and exuberant—
but now each of you is spread out in his own
territory of pain, two steps per inhale, two per exhale,
up the hot scree, occasional hands for balance or for torque,
sometimes a pause to switch a little weight,
one shoulder to the other.

You notice your breath;
it's what you're reduced to, counterpoint to the feet.
And you think about your heart,
its muscled, glossy flanks.

Breathe out all the way to ease a knot
in the back or calf, the way only an exhale can,
into all the sinews and ravines....
Like any body fully asleep, this body soldiers up into itself.

Do you need only what you have,
have only what you need?
Another false ridge is approaching,
like a watermelon with its black teeth.

Is the lake a cold beer, a kiss like you've never had?
Shadow or Gem or Aloha,
Lucille or Susie or June.
The lake is a lake.
Cold in October, for swimming or mosquitoes.
And sentinel to the sudden falls, straight down,
the gnarled, massive cedars will endure
another thousand years of snow.

Clouds and Sunset

I

A mastodon,
a wild boar on its wing—

and those—giant Labradors pulling
glaciers back to the pole

II

A rush toward the sun
from both directions.

Then like that the eye
splits, winks

and we're only backlit now—
furry honey

III

A corpse floats
across the sky—

where the sun used to be,
an anvil

shivering

IV

The ocean has become
the Zhou dynasty

distant, practically hidden,
endless trees,

strong emperors, many kingdoms
unraveling—

and as a shark becomes an orchid
a snake appears from a raven's jaw.

V

They're passing the corpse
over themselves now.

He has a top-knot
a funny snout

a very long bier.
It is dissolving—

with all the buddies,
the whole orchestra.

Not far, cerebral cortex
from *vas deferens*—

third eye
to asshole.

Just a little uplift

VI

amid shades of green and rose,
but all you feel entirely

sure of is: 1) that muskrat
is writing in Arabic and

2) those other rats
are standing progressively upright

in the gloam

VII

just grey on grey now,
a silhouette—a long ink-blot

VIII

when everything else is gone,
how slowly and soundlessly they carry

Pharaoh Khafra—
or is it the great sphinx of Giza?

his regal headdress,
and mane of tangled mist—

back out over the long black sea.

First Massage
For Robin Fann

I knew I would feel relaxed, even voluptuous...
but the little kick of grief surprised me.
Midwife of kindness!
So this is what we forget
in our dailiness.
You took my liver-spotted hands—
they were a friend's hands;
lifted and turned each leg—twisted haunches—
worked each toe, the leathery sole. What's left?
Everything's thrumming—we must be done.

That's when you took the back of the neck,
moved gently across
head, face, to the receding
hairline, forehead where starlight
leapt between your fingers.

Then one hand on heart,
another just below the stomach:
bass tones, a triad...
but I'm not going to close with a riff
about the music of the chakras
although they are music, and you
make them sing.

When I was your age and
a nursing assistant
for the better part of a year,
well, this morning, I remembered,
in your hands, other hands...

the intimate touch
of some of those strangers, my patients:
like rubbing the back of the stroke victim who

spoke only anymore in plural nouns,
or turning the obese patient
with another nurse and sponge-bathing her
one side at a time for a little longer than we were supposed to...
secreting in some respect or tenderness

for a person in shame, or dread—
so even if they knew we were just paid
to cheer them up, they also felt something
else we left them with—
something no one is ever paid well enough for.

                    *

The body ages.
It takes a turn
for the worse, and then today,
my aging body...
your hands...
your skill and tenderness.
Whitman said to love the body

for what it is,
and love it well...
to know the spirit and the body
are wrapped in one sweet cloth.
And gratitude—each day
to hoist that banner and pass it forward
across the bloody world.

III

Anything on Earth

Flesh Music

I put a hand against the piano
while you play Brahms:
high strings in the fingertips,
bass notes in the palm,

warm against the ringing cherry chest.
Better than seeing sunlight
is feeling it, holding
the whale's flanks.

It's flesh music, a sunlit room...
Father's accordion, Mother's song.
Ocean womb:
My son and I ride the waves

along the river mouth, feel
the music all day long.

Spring Retreat
Logos, New Camaldoli Hermitage, Lucia

For three days, you look down on ocean and fog
from a trailer deck of weathered planks, its trellis roof laden
with blooming wisteria. She's taken over—her vine brocade
chuppa, her odor of a lover's skin, is the very air
you breathe, embroidered shawl come to life in a dream.
Oh, you're learning to love your grandiose little self...
and yes, you're distracted while you're here by many thoughts.
But could you, could anyone, hope to dance as well in the mind
as this wisteria?
                You sweep and marvel, marvel, sweep—
or don't sweep—let the petals and buds snow down randomly
onto your clothes, your books, your hair, into your eyes
and form their chaos at your feet like a fragrant carpet
of purpled snow. And when dawn rings the small chimes and petals,
standing in the sensory space, how you go from plant to man, to blossom—
1-2-3 just like that—three short bows, the time is gone.

Thanksgiving
for David Aquino

When you can't breathe at all
there's a long crowning
minute or so before the lungs start to really burn
when, as in comedy, you may stumble
out the kitchen door, a fish out of water

to where David is measuring for a deck rail;
he takes in your ballet, its demi-wheezes and wide eyes,
luckily a language he can read,
and then you're being flipped around
heimliched—he's remarking on each decision—
he's done this sort of thing before, more than once,
on jobsites, boats: a tuna fisherman
choking on a tuna sandwich,
an electrocuted worker (who died, you later hear).

So next when David tells you to lie down flat
and try to relax, pounds you on the back
by the heel of his open palm, it's sort of comforting,
although you still can't breathe,
and any time now that minute of grace will end.
So he asks if he should call 911,
which is certainly the right question;
he's tried what he knows
and is not finding you much of a conversationalist.
It's time to pick up the phone.

You are at a remove, appreciative,
but your gaze seems to you
to originate from somewhere high above
your right eyebrow. I mean, it's comic, right?
the wheezing, and stranger still,
the not being able to wheeze.

How long can this go on,
from what, a corn chip?
the karmic fate of a multi-tasker
who seems to have wanted to save a few minutes
by breathing, eating, and pacing around
balancing his checkbook all at the same time.

You could alert your wife
at the front of the house—
lope and stagger in there suffocating
where she is teaching piano to small children.
No, have David tell her
after he grabs the phone.
He pounds your back one more time;
you stay face down,
like the call to prayer—
you think: you're even facing east.

And that's as far as it goes this time—
just a glimpse; not the full dark fury.
Is it the jarring, or just
the lying down and totally relaxing
releases the cramped valve?
Like waking from a little dream,
the wheezing dissipates,
the channel opens, and the body respires,

inspires, prostrate to new redwood 2 x 6,
inhaling the sawdust of this new day,
which indeed, upon reflection,
has a remarkable patina
as you think, "Where was I?
Where *am* I! Who am I?"
pulled dying of thirst off the lifeboat,
then flopped up living on David's brand new ship.

The Gardener
For Kit

You get down on your knees in the dark earth—alone
for hours in hot sun, yanking weed roots, staking trellises,
burning your shoulders, swatting gnats; you strain your muscled
midwestern neck and back, callous your pianist's hands.

You cut roses back so they won't fruit, rip out and replace
spent annuals. You fill your garden dense with roots and vines.
And when a humble sprout climbs like a worm up out of death,
you are there to bless it, in your green patch, all spring and summer long,

hose like a scepter, a reliquary vessel; you hum
through the dreamy wilderness—no one to judge, absolve,
or be absolved—purified by labor, confessed by its whisperings, connected
to its innocence. So when you heft a woody, brushy tangle, or stumble

inside grimy, spent by earth, I see all the sacraments in place—
and the redeemed world never smelled so sweet.

The Promise

Eight orange quarters glowing on a plate.
I have sliced them as a way to anticipate.
I will eat them when the sun goes down.
I have exacted their promise. But more than that,

I have moved the wedges to the round edge
and rotated it slowly in front of my face
where each in turn offers its truth, its
diaphanous beaded citrus curtain into the divine.

I never deserved this and never shall;
what the nose tells is how good they are.
What I say is that they are mine. But not yet. Later.
Because the promise of a thing is almost as good

as the thing itself. Maybe better. And in the not having
comes light setting the orange afire, comes
fragrance, a voice saying *please* or *yes.*
Comes a sweeter taste. Comes song.

Echo Space
The Castle Ruin at Saissac

You sing an arpeggio, a ninth chord,
and it hangs there a long time.
Here is the beauty of the human face.

Almost any room is a cathedral.
No one around, not even guards
in the twelve centuries of rubble.

So many strands converge;
you sing pentatonic scales—
whole-tones leave us

dreamy again, as if there were a harp.
The charm of impossibilities. I'm imagining
a piano; someone's arm across the keys

or random notes, with the pedal down.
That's what the stars are like, held onto
above Black Mountain—*the Montagne Noire.*

And when you laugh, there it is,
the full strange chord of your laughter,
unmistakable, a true thing,

its own force in the vaulted room,
long after you stop your song,
long after you close your eyes.

Final Boarding
John Lovas, 1940-2005

What journey is this?
I don't know, John,
but I know you
have faced the world
openly,
inelegantly,
like almost every animal
I admire most.

Sorry, I can't think
of a sophisticated
literary reference,
only a certain
strangeness,
like a poetry walk
without you in it.

Or shall we
shut up?
Not say we love you?
Not say you are laureate
of these green hills?
Not stand here
and be late for whatever's
on the schedule?
Yeah, why not skip
everything,
just huddle together
as the sun moves
into twilight,
talk a little among
ourselves.

That's the ticket,
isn't it, John;
say it: and even
after it dissolves
into song, pure sound,
into phatic
dust,
say it,
and mean it.

The Beauty of Work as a Boy

It must be done.
You'll be sticky and scrubbing at sap
all week in the shower
before reaching for the mineral spirits
to distinguish you back among the soft skinned.

You'll have the hair of a saint or a madman,
strewn with sawdust, leaf fragments, twigs, thorns,
oils of the thickets and sweat from the back of your hands
and your face, bruised, swathed, decorated
with the great pigment earth.

You'll have bark and sharp leaves in your gloves and socks,
down your long sleeves.

You'll have little gashes and itches,
achy fingers and a heavy-sore right arm

from hefting the chain saw
on those steep hillsides;
shake out the head scarf at the end of the day....

You'll have cleaned what stood to burn you out,
what stood uninvited, the weedy eucalyptus crowns,

and limping home
that kind of innocence—unkempt, unaware—
someone looks hard at you.
There might be a man in you yet.

Painting Job

A neighbor has given me a job
because my father is dead.
I'm hand-painting a house for his friend.
These are kind people—the owner, his friend;
they never knew my father,
but they know our situation.

Two weeks have passed
and I've slowly painted the whole east side
the dark desired green with off-white trim
and held in wonder the heft of a week's cash pay.
Now more than two stories high,
reaching out under the eaves,
I remind myself not to panic or lunge
if anything starts to teeter.

I'd never studied mindfulness or breathing,
nor the tai chi of leaning—just baseball.
Now sideways against the ladder rungs,
bucket pullied and propped precariously
on its flimsy sloping tray,

I travel out to the gutter's edge
then inward to just above my smeared face
and spotted glasses—learning to work,
hoping for this mild break in earthquakes
to continue. Counting on a little luck.

And who were these people—a neighbor, a stranger—
paying me for this clumsy effort, sincere,
mistake-filled (did he want the eaves' undersides
painted green or white? or not at all?)
I saw him squint a long time looking.

Rare Bob Dylan

For James O'Keefe (1955-2008)

Three visits while you were sick, just the two of us:
a classic National League baseball game;
a symphony concert, during which you noticed
you weren't reading the program as well as you should,
a sign that the cancer could be spreading...

then driving you to Berkeley for an appointment
and eating at "Little Africa," that meal
of yams, plantains, beans, chicken, and spicy rice.
We talked Chinese art, the brilliance of *Mad* Magazine,
of your endless union fights on behalf of teachers,
and what it was like to not be sure when you were going to die.

And then the mental snapshot: you're seated back
on your couch with your new recordings—you've been enjoying
music more than ever—today it's rare Bob Dylan. I take my leave
and we exchange a look that says in an instant—
an unmeasurable amount of time—that we live
in a world of meaning—and there you are, in mine,
as a few months later, at a band rehearsal,

playing Grieg's *Funeral March* on French Horn 3,
it becomes clear to me after just four bars that you are also
enjoying this intense, highly wrought progression—
collaborator, truly present, now on the other side of the mystery,
watching us grapple with our instruments so earnestly:
to play in tune, do justice to our anthems for the dying and the dead,
but really for our own steadfast courage—each hello, goodbye—
this instant: your spirit—your passion for the world—as a guide.

Dear Maude,

I'm sitting down to eat these pretty good quesadillas
with sweet onion, cilantro and this really
tangy new Mexican sauce
when the phone rings and on the message

I'm hearing how you died last night,
so of course I pick up, talk to our friend a while,
then return to table a little in shock now
where the food has turned to stone.

Though right away I hear you saying,
"Eat! eat"—"I wish I could join!"—
"They don't let me eat a thing anymore!"—
and laughing about it.

It seems you're right here in the living room,
your warmth welling up, your belief
in the dignity and good intentions
of all our labors, and all who struggle to survive.

And then I'm also thinking: who picked the cilantro—
cooled the Vidalia onions, kept them dry—processed
the endless tortillas—who is home with *their* children,
who'll cook for *them*, take them to the doctor?

You won't stop your smiling as I slouch and brood
with the guilt of the living. You're just there,
a mother who has very reasonable expectations,
who says "Eat," says: "Now you're pissing me off,"

says: "I'll be watching," says: "Do something with your life."

—Maude Meehan 1920 – 2007

Singing Fire
for the Wendt family

Tonight a child will build and light the ritual campfire
with one match. You taught him this: not to be afraid,
sing fire into being, eyes reverent upon it. He plans with care
a way to reach the innermost bed of madrone bark curls:
to lie flat and slide a hand, then his breath, all the way in
to the tender nest of crackling moss, parched maple leaves,
certain to hiss and catch the tiny bundle of crisp oak twigs,
then reach out above those first smoky longings—
and spark the next layer, a cabin of thumb-size branches
before breaking through to the outermost teepee
where split oak and madrone ignite and blaze
to mad heat—all the way through to the last song.

Pacific Moonsets

1.
Frayed moon,
mandarin free-fall to the color of embers,
coals aching,
sinking now like a burning ship.
So far away, there was nothing I could do.

2.
Feline, heavy lidded,
in no hurry
to remove its gaze—
for a long time,
a cradle in the ficus limbs.

3.
Fire, stone, water,
chill night air,
and a hunger I cannot name.
Did I close my eyes?
Who swallowed it so quickly?

Creation

When the tide is high,
water comes all the way to here...
covers the sandy bed,
laps against those weeds
with its salt blood—

You used to play
in that gully with your friends,
the muck and the weeds.

Mozart sits alone in a quiet room
and there is a kind of love
of who he is—his essence,
his three-year-old glee
at discovering triads—
that never goes away,
that has nothing,
will never have
anything—anyone;

it is an absence,
a father's love,
unfillable.

Listening to Ives

Emily Dickinson
is going nearly the speed of light.
Desmond Tutu is with her.
They're in a train.
It's a theoretical
physics problem—
do they ever get old? It's also
a word problem.
How far away are they?
It's heartbreaking, the railroad.

We can't keep up.
Brutal
music frames
the second strophe,
another overheard
hymn distorted
as if buried and uncovered
by a piano in
another century.

It's scratchy autopsy—
the present, the past,
the even farther past.
Yet somehow the fractured
music transfigures
its own lament,
exuberance
haunted now
by history
as by tenderness.

I Am No Sufi

But sometimes
I spin
in the space
of love's absence,

dizzy like the sisters
in Chekhov,
spinning around
the orchard they must leave

forever—you do not
claim what is
unclaimable. She
does not own

the sweet orchards.
I do not own
my sons.
I cannot help them

when they are away
and grown.
But in the dream
of a spinning

universe
I can let my dizziness
play like a necessary wine,
and the words

can mimic at last
the ghost that is
my knowing…
and wanting…

and I can be
a little humbler then
since as I spin
I am every father

determined to be
his son's
good angel—
his child's second skin.

How to Make Sense

the normal shadow
across the bed...

the morning light and wind
moving the curtains...

a little bacon frying

        *

that evening you make plans
all the way to the end

of the barbecue

you cry then

        *

listening to something
only you can hear

        *

and when the ground
is suddenly
useless, except to lie down...

you lie down
in the grass

        *

sometimes,

the fact is
organic things
are bad enough,

but almost every inorganic thing
can just go to hell.

*

the mind
is a chrysalis. so
what?

the evening brings
its glass of wine....

you read
a book

you hungered for

what were you thinking

*

it feels good
the next day
just to run
to the bank, the cleaners

with your college-age
son
hear the voices

of people
who don't know

you're in earshot....

someone's

got to vacuum,
there is cleaning

all sorts of plans

to be made....
Whenever
you feel up to it,

dear

    *

or at night,

in the chest...

the broad hole
the moon makes

    *

and then the
ghost again...

there's no

hurrying
the twilight
the dusk

    *

how to go
to sleep
on this raft

surrounded by
thirst...

*

suddenly
awake

what was it you
forgot,

surely
something

fixable, something

that will get
done,
can be
undone....

*

salt spray
sweeps a billion years
beneath the moon.

you ride

the time.

you hold on to
something

no one else knows,

something no one else
will ever know

you had.

Anything on Earth

E non ho amato mai tanto la vita!
And never have I loved life so much! — Mario Cavardossi
"E lucevan le stele" from *Tosca* by Giocamo Puccini

The solo clarinet
in Act III of *Tosca*—
you can barely see him

from the upper right dress circle
(although you can spit on the box seats
from there). Tonight he is a young prodigy

from Russia, guessing by his name
in the program, and he looks
like a schoolboy swaying a little

in the dark pit, the only mover
among the statuesque rapture
of his proximate colleagues....

They have done this work
all their adult lives, but tonight you can
see their halfway smiles

glowing a little among stand lights.
You can feel them listening.
He must have been this gorgeous every night so far.

Even the conductor's hand is
held within the spell,
not from the famed tenor, but from,

barely visible, the back reaches of the band.
The lover writes to Tosca
one last time. She'll soon sing again

of her doomed hope. You will love her;
in fact, you may *be* in love with her.
But his is the truest longing,

the so oft-unsung
song beneath the song—
that pours now from the eternally young heart,

pure sympathy from underneath
all the unstoppable hullabaloo:
lust, betrayal, greed.

Offstage music
that loves regardless, despite
knowing what will come of us.

Puccini must have understood this
when he gave his most beautiful moment
not to one of his well-known lovers, but to

the clarinet, far removed from the makeup and spotlight,
shadowed among cork grease, valve oil,
spit swabs and split reeds:

how the archetype is as real
as the instinct; how the music
holds the meaning up—holds us all up—

says this moment, some sixteen bars in slow three,
from underneath, from the clarinet,
is as real and unspeakable as anything on earth.

A Proclamation Concerning a Bowl of Apples

Whereas they command the space in my room
like offerings in the arched casement light

Whereas they show pomegranate highlights and saffron shadings
stem-end, blossom-end, equally haphazard, and fortunate

Whereas they rained down on my head in the picking
quickly filled the basket
and sometimes fit into my hands two or three at a time like baseballs

Whereas they are beautiful in their patience

Whereas they are the gift of the gift of an immigrant farmer
that farmer is no longer with us
and his trees don't care which side of the fence they hang down on

Whereas my knife is sharp

Whereas they are red in more ways than one
mottled and golden and penumbral
it is harvest, and each longs to be touched

Whereas it's what they live for
what we live for

Whereas there is thunder and sweet gaping
and it is our teeth and wild jaw splits open the tree

Whereas we too shall be eaten
by love, by eyes, by fire, by worms—

Let it hereby be resolved
to savor the presence

of apples, the absence of apples
the very idea of apples

in a bowl, on a windowsill, in autumn.

Ken Weisner is a poet, editor, and teacher living in Santa Cruz. He is originally from Oakland, a graduate of Skyline High School. He received his BA in English from Oberlin College, an MFA in Poetry Writing from the Iowa Writer's Workshop, and a PhD in Comparative Literature from UC Santa Cruz. Between 1984 and 1999, Ken edited *Quarry West* Magazine through Porter College at UCSC. He currently edits *Red Wheelbarrow* through De Anza Community College in Cupertino, where he teaches literature, composition, and creative writing. His first book of poems, *The Sacred Geometry of Pedestrians*, was published by Hummingbird Press in 2002. Ken has also worked as a poet-in-the-schools throughout the Central Coast, and is an avid hobbyist on the French horn. He lives with his wife, the pianist and potter Kit Birskovich. They have two grown sons.